Emotion
and
Psyche

Emotion and Psyche

Marc Jackson

BOOKS

Winchester, UK
Washington, USA

First published by O-Books, 2010
O Books is an imprint of John Hunt Publishing Ltd., The Bothy, Deershot Lodge, Park Lane, Ropley,
Hants, SO24 0BE, UK
office1@o-books.net
www.o-books.com

For distributor details and how to order please visit the 'Ordering' section on our website.

Text copyright Marc Jackson 2009

ISBN: 978 1 84694 378 2

A CIP catalogue record for this book is available from the British Library.

Design: Stuart Davies

Printed in the UK by CPI Antony Rowe
Printed in the USA by Offset Paperback Mfrs, Inc

We operate a distinctive and ethical publishing philosophy in all
areas of its business, from its global network of authors to
production and worldwide distribution.

CONTENTS

Introduction

The purpose of this work is to explain an entire world view. It is a world view built on an emotion-based psyche. As such it will explain its view of emotions, and building upon them describe an explanation of the world. It will start with describing the experience of emotions, and what the work means by an emotion. The work will then explain the dynamics of those emotions, that is how they function in the human psyche. With the dynamics of the human psyche described, emotion's role in explaining the world will be described. An emotion-based ethic will be described. Lastly the emotional relations between people will be examined. As such it is both a work of philosophy and psychology. It is a world philosophy built upon an account of the psyche.

The work will attempt to present this emotion-based world view in an effective manner. Leaving it to the reader to decide from their own experience whether the account of the world given is accurate or not.

The method used to expound this world view will be one of description rather than argument. Description of experience. For the world view is based upon experience, and is made sound by the confirmation of that experience by repeated experience. The reader will often be invited not to take the work's word for what it describes but to experience it themselves, and confirm it first-hand. With the emphasis on experience it might be tempting to call this a work of science but to do so would be misleading. This is not because of any lack of rigor on the work's part, but because what is usually called science is primarily sensual. That is, science is understood to be based upon experience provided by the five senses. As the main experiences of this work are not sensual but emotional it would therefore be misleading to call it science.

If it is not, properly speaking, science what is the work's standard of evidence? As will be seen, the standard of evidence comes out from the work itself. This standard of evidence is experience centered truth. This cannot yet be explained but part of its meaning can be hinted at, that it is not a work of the imagination, or an abstract reasoning but grounded and centered upon experience. This criteria of evidence has been retrospectively applied to the entire work.

Part I

Description

Chapter 1

What is an emotion?

This work has its own thoughts about what an emotion is. In order to understand that, preconceptions of what emotions are need to be put aside. The use of emotion in this work is of course related to the normal use of the word, but with its own more defined meaning. In the description of emotions that will be given thinking, "That's not what an emotion is," will be of no use. Similarly, in the descriptions of emotions that are to come it will be of no use if the reader thinks when reading the description of an emotion something like, "I think that actually that is irritation not anger." Such preconceptions must be dispensed with if the work is to be understood. More important than any arguing over labels is the experience of the underlying phenomena which the labels are trying to refer to. When what is an emotion is described the important part is not the name given to it, but whether the description of the underlying experiences is accurate or not.

Emotions are felt. Felt in the sense of experienced as a feeling. Sorrow is not tears and sighs, it is a feeling that the person experiencing it feels. It is that feeling that makes it an emotion, not the expression (which is an expression of the underlying feeling). If a robot could be made that could imitate crying and the facial expressions usually associated with sorrow it would none the less not be experiencing sorrow. Like the experience of pain is more than a cry of "Ow!", so emotions as this work calls them are feelings. Not feelings in the same sense as pain which is connected with the sense of touch, but in a related sense. The reader can check this for themselves, if they think of something frightening and experience that fear then I expect they will find that they feel that fear. Nor is that feeling just something physical like a clenching of the stomach or a lift in the pulse rate; it is a distinct feeling in addition to those. This feeling of emotions as will be seen is very important. The physical expressions and associations will turn out to be changeable and not always present; the feeling of the emotion though will remain. It is the emotion as the feeling, not the expression, that this work considers the emotion. As such what will be used to distinguish between emotions is not their various expressions but their difference in feeling tone.

Emotions motivate. They stimulate "motion". In other words they motivate action (as well as inaction). For example when a person feels angry it may motivate them to lash out, or when a person is afraid it may make them rooted to the spot. This is why I have chosen to call what I am describing emotions rather than feelings or any other term. They are that which motivates a person. A person may have a whole list of reasons for doing something but the stimulus for them actually carrying it out will be an emotion. For example to me this description is incomplete: "The child cried because his mother took the toy away." It has left out the emotion that stimulated the child to cry. Emotions are that which motivate at the most basic level. Basic in the sense of the underlying cause. At the bottom of every action will be an emotion that is motivating it. Thus to return to the example: "The child cried because the mother took the toy away," because this made it upset, and, "The mother took the toy away," because she was angry. Moreover when the motivating emotion is found it is also basic in the sense that no further cause is needed. The mother may have been angry because she had had a bad day at the office, but for the motivation of the taking the toy away all that was needed was the anger. To add any more would be to over explain. Thus when asking why a person ran away it is enough to say that they were afraid, to add that they were afraid because they felt threatened is not necessary. For example a person may be afraid of moths; their behavior in regard to moths can be explained by them feeling afraid; an extra rationalization that this fear is because they feel moths threaten them is unnecessary. Enough has been said when the emotion that motivates has been recognized.

Emotions can be experienced primordially.[1] That is they can be experienced in an unmediated way (primordial: at the start, first). When one experiences them it is not like with one of the five senses where you are experiencing sense data rather than the object (like a person who is short-sighted seeing something at distance sees it distorted), but is accessed directly. There is no intermediary experienced between the emotion felt and the emotion experienced. The emotion can be experienced by itself. There does not have to be an accompanying thought or action in order to experience it. Experience shows this, for example I can feel sad without being sad about anything or doing anything, in that case I am just sad. The reader can test this for themselves from their own experience. Emotions can be experienced by themselves as themselves. As such when building upon emotions one can build on them alone as there is no intermediary.

Therefore an emotion is felt, unmediated by anything else, and it motivates. The next step is to list them. This presents a particular problem because of the problems of language, and also that emotions are usually experienced by the individual alone. In the sense that, unlike in a biological matter, one cannot point to the emotion being experienced such that other people can examine it and agree that it is that emotion. This does not mean that communication about emotions is impossible but that it is difficult. It is possible because we all have them so that through dialogue we can agree that two people have the same emotion and are talking about the same emotion. It is difficult because different people will use different words to label the same felt emotion. For example what one person might call anxiety another calls worry. A further difficulty is that two or more emotions can be experienced at once, thus we must distinguish between one emotion and what are multiple emotions.

The method that can be used to distinguish between emotions has already presented itself given what emotions are, that is they can be distinguished on the basis of whether they feel different. It is on that basis of feeling tone that they will be distinguished. The list given will be based on my own experience; I strongly recommend that the reader check the list for themselves for the list is not definite or infallible, it could be changed in the light of new experience or the reconsideration of experience. This is the list:

Love: this is the feeling of affection not the feeling of sex, the kind of feeling you might get when you think with affection of your mother or spouse

Kindness: this is a positive feeling, a feeling of benevolence, it feels similar to love but different, you might get it when you give to someone out of kindness

Joy: this is a really uplifting feeling, you might get it when you receive good news or are having a good time

Faith: feels positive, like a good expectation, you might get it when you trust that something good is going to happen, a looking-forward feeling

Awe: this is a feeling of wonder, you might experience it when you look with wonder at the stars or at a sunset, in that way it is associated with finding something beautiful

Pity: is like a combination of love and sorrow but I think it is separate rather than those two emotions experienced at once, you might experience it when you hear a sad tale and think something like "poor thing" or "aah"

Respect: is a feeling of positive admiration, like a feeling of looking up to someone in a wholesome way

Reason: is a feeling of thinking, chewing something over, meditating on it

Guilt: the feeling of having done something wrong, a

burdensome feeling, in some ways similar to worry

Disgust: not the physical disgust but the kind of feeling often associated with "eew I don't approve of that", when one is disgusted with somebody else, revolted by something

Embarrassment: the feeling when some people blush or you squirm because somebody else is making a fool of themselves or you think you yourself are, an uncomfortable feeling

Sorrow: the feeling of sadness, you might experience it when a loved one dies, or when you are depressed

Worry: a tense feeling, like when one is worried that you forgot to turn the gas off or something like that

Want: want as in a feeling of desire, like hunger or thirst, a basic feeling, like looking at someone else eating and feeling you want to eat too

Fear: the feeling of being scared, frightened

Sex drive: that feeling of desire, different to want, the feeling of being turned on or up for it

Curiosity: a feeling of "I wonder what that is" or "what does that do", or of overhearing a conversation and wanting to know what it's about

Amusement: the feeling of laughter and smiling, when one finds something funny, it is different to the feeling of joy, it is not so high

Belief: a feeling that something is so, like a premonition or a commitment, a feeling of a kind of certainty

Anger: like a lightning flash, a lashing-out feeling, or yelling feeling

Hate: different to anger, a brooding loathing, simmers rather than boils

Greed: different to want, a possessive wanting more feeling

Vanity: a puffed up feeling, inflated feeling, superior feeling

Envy: that feeling often associated with being jealous of someone, like a hate but different

Cruelty: a destructive feeling, a hurting-others feeling

Naturally it has been necessary to be rather poetic in describing the feelings. It is best if the reader experiences them for themselves, actually feels them rather than just thinks about them. The associations mentioned are common but not universal. Emotions are not tied down to being felt about certain things or motivating only certain things. For example feeling sorrow is not confined to being felt over something lost. However, the human race does have some common patterns to what their feelings are felt over.

Chapter 2

Categories

The reader may have noticed that the emotions as listed are sometimes similar in feeling and sometimes not. Based on how they feel they can be categorized into four groups. The first group consists of love, kindness, joy, faith, awe, and pity; they all have a similar high feeling, high as in uplifting. The second group consists of reason, guilt, disgust, worry, embarrassment, sorrow and respect; they all have a similar pulling away/withdrawing feeling to them. Respect has some of the high feeling of the first group but I think has more of the withdrawn feeling of the second group. The third group consists of want, fear, the sex drive, curiosity, amusement, belief and anger; they all have a similar direct feeling to them, that is a thrusting-out feeling. Anger has the direct feeling but also has some of the feeling of the fourth group, I think it has more of the direct though. The fourth group consists of hate, greed, vanity, envy and cruelty; they all have a similar violent/bitter feeling, a sharp feeling. Hate has similarities with anger but they do feel different; hate feels more deep down and anger more thrusting out. Greed has similarities with want but greed has a more grasping, grabbing feeling. The reader must decide for themselves whether they fit into those groups; however, the groups do feel fairly distinct even though some emotions are a little ambiguous. The groups as outlined should help the reader obtain a better grasp of what was trying to be communicated in the description of the separate emotions.

The categories mentioned it must be noted are not just different expressions of four primary emotions. They have a similar feeling but are not the same; in fact there is a wide diversity within them that shows they are separate. For example curiosity feels very different but none the less similar to fear. Emotions remain as the most basic level; they cannot be broken down any further.

The first thing to notice about the categories is some are distinct to humans whereas some are common to both humans and animals. This is a tricky area as our perceptions of animals are prejudiced by our projections onto them. Nor can they be consulted in dialogue about what emotions they experience. I think the first and fourth groups above are only experienced by humans, whereas the second and third groups are experienced by animals. I think without projection the second and third groups can be observed (as far as that is possible) in animals but the first and fourth cannot. Love and hate etc. are often attributed to animals but in the prescribed terms of this work I think that they cannot be said to be shown. Whereas emotions from the third category like curiosity, want, the sex drive etc. seem to be clearly shown by animals. Reason, guilt, respect etc., the emotions of the second category, seem to be shown by some animals (dogs, cats, some birds) but not all. This experience helps with dividing the categories as an extra mode of division can be employed, namely whether animals exhibit the emotions. For example animals seem to show anger thus this confirms that it is a third category emotion, and animals also seem to show respect (which could also be called loyalty) confirming it as a second category emotion.

The second category consisting of reason, guilt, disgust, worry, embarrassment, sorrow and respect is called by this work neutral. The third category consisting of want, fear, sex drive, curiosity, amusement, belief and anger is called natural. This is to reflect their status with animals.

Chapter 3

Primordial Conflicts

There are two groups left to label. They are the two distinctly human groups consisting of love and hate etc. The thing that stands out for these two groups is the conflict between them. If you try to feel an emotion from each group at once you will experience a conflict, a tension between them. In a way they do not want to be felt together. For example if you try to feel love and hate at the same time you can feel the tension. This is unique to feeling these two groups at the same time; if you feel an emotion from another group with one of them there is no tension. This tension is primordial to them; it is not felt because of anything else; in order to experience it you just need to feel the opposing emotions. This tension is not an emotion, it does not motivate nor is it basic; it is a by-product of feeling these two opposing groups of emotions at the same time.

Opposing emotions; that is how the two unlabeled human groups will be labeled, as opposites. The first group consisting of love, kindness, joy, faith, awe and pity is good. I call it this because of its high feeling and because it consists of what is normally called good. If I wanted to say what good is, these emotions would be it. They are good. They are not called good because they motivate good actions but because they themselves are good. The fourth group consisting of hate, greed, vanity, envy and cruelty is evil. I call it this because of its violent/bitter feeling and because these things are normally called evil. Moreover if I wanted to say what evil is these emotions would be it. They are evil. They are not called evil because they motivate evil actions but because they themselves are evil.

The two remaining groups are good and evil. They are the

human only groups. The four categories are good, neutral, natural and evil.

Chapter 4

Action Conflicts

A primordial conflict has already been discussed; the main thing to distinguish this from is action conflicts. An action conflict is when two or more emotions motivate a different course over a given action. One emotion may be motivating the person to do a certain action while another is motivating them not to do it, or one emotion may be motivating a person to do one thing about something and another a different thing. For example someone who is dieting may want to eat a slice of cake; the emotion want motivating for eating and the emotion reason for not eating. Thus the conflict is not primordial but over a given action. Again someone might feel anger at an insult and want to lash out, but at the same time not want to lash out because they are afraid they will be hit back. Another example would be someone who has to decide which course of action to follow at a certain time. Do they follow guilt and mend the fence or do they follow curiosity and watch the football results? Thus an action conflict is when two or more emotions disagree on a course of action and thereby conflict over it. The conflict only lasts as long as the two emotions push in different directions over the given action. Resolution is achieved when one emotion overpowers the other or when the possibility of action goes away. In the lashing out example, if the person who may be lashed out at apologizes the motivational struggle that is going on might end. There could be a series of action conflicts (like in the diet example for instance), but each specific conflict would be an action conflict not the whole. It is important to note that an action conflict can occur with the same emotion on both sides of the argument as it were. For example a man might feel attracted to two women at a party and be pulled in different directions by the sex drive as to which one to approach.

This helps explain the primordial conflict between good and evil. Good and evil are not simply motivating different courses of action but are in conflict anyway. Moreover that conflict is permanent, not just for as long as the deliberation over an action continues.

Action conflicts explain much. Conscience can be thought of as an action conflict. In the sense that when a person has a moment of conscience over whether they should do something that they might consider wrong they have different emotions pulling in different directions. Indecision can also be explained by action conflicts as the person hesitates because they are being motivated in different directions.

Chapter 5

Difference

The emotions that have been described are not just there when they are active and felt now, but are there to be drawn upon. For example fear is not only in me when I feel it in the present, but is there in me to be activated in the future as it has been in the past. A stockpile of emotion to be drawn upon, that can either become active or remain inactive. Emotions can be either active, or inactive with the potential to become active.

Experience shows emotions can be experienced at different strengths. For instance one experience of kindness can be more strongly felt than another prior experience. An emotion can be felt more or less strongly at a given time. For example a dog suddenly barking could make me feel fear slightly while a horror film could give a feeling of fear that is stronger and more intense than the fear felt when the dog barked. Thus emotions are felt sometimes stronger and sometimes weaker. The reader can check this from their own experience.

People have different emotional compositions. Some people for example are angrier or more frightened than others in general. For example one person may have as their dominant emotions reason and curiosity and show a lack of fear and anger while a different person may have the sex drive as their dominant emotion and show a lack of worry and reason. People are composed of different strengths of emotions; they show emotions in them that are stronger or weaker than their other emotions, and they will have different strengths compared to other people.

Experience shows that people's emotional composition changes over time. In the sense that someone may have a sorrowful period of life or an angry period of life and then change. For example a child may be very greedy in their early years but then get less greedy as they get older. Thus people's emotional compositions are not static; but it is shown by experience that they can alter with time.

This change over time can be explained. It seems from experience that there is a connection between the frequent feeling of an emotion and the increase of that emotion overall in a person. Similarly the lack of use of an emotion seems to be connected with the diminishing of an emotion in a person. For example if someone keeps becoming angry they change into being a more angry person. Likewise if a person does not feel love as often as in the past they will have less love lying inactive in them to be drawn upon in the future, and will thus be less loving.

A person's emotional make-up then changes with use; if an emotion is used more it grows, if it is used less it diminishes, and if it is used the same it remains the same. Emotions can grow and diminish in a person. This growth is accomplished by activity. Like a muscle the more an emotion is used the bigger it becomes; the less it is used the smaller it becomes. Active use of an emotion affects the amount of that emotion which lies inactive within that person. In order to be maintained an emotion must become active in some form; if it remains inactive it will diminish.

This growth of emotions raises the question of how this growth is possible. A muscle draws on nutrients to grow, what does an emotion draw upon? A pool of psychic energy needs to be supposed in some form to explain this growth. Whether this pool is physical or to do with the brain is yet to be answered. At the moment it is just a pool of energy that is formless until it is formed into an emotion. When an emotion is activated it draws upon this pool of psychic energy; the longer and more intensely the emotion is activated the greater the draw on the pool, and the more energy is converted into that emotion.

Part II

Dynamics

Chapter 6

Associations

Experience shows that emotions are not just floating free within us but form associations with people and things. For example someone might associate sorrow with the color blue, love with their spouse, or sexual desire with the breasts. Association is not just meant in an abstract sense but in a direct feeling sense, like a person with the association of sorrow with blue becoming depressed when they are left in a room that is painted blue. In that sense the association is a trigger to the emotion; it has sparked off an emotion. These associations can range from the simple, like associating cheeseburgers with want, to the complex, like a bench being associated with their grandmother who they remember telling them a pleasant story on it when they were little which triggers emotions of sorrow and amusement when they see it. Emotions are not bound only to certain associations; one could potentially associate any emotion with anything.

These associations are shown by experience to build up with frequent use or a strong experience. For example a theme tune to a favorite program will build up an association over time, whereas a fear of dogs might come from one powerfully bad experience. The reader can check this for themselves from their own experience of associations. Just like with the growth of an emotion, use is of paramount importance to our associations (after all, what is underpinning them is emotion). An association that is not used will fade in time; similarly an association that is triggered more frequently will grow in strength.

Some of these associations are sensual, deriving from the body. For example the stomach rumbling being associated with want, or a certain time of the month with the sex drive. Thus there are sensual associations that have triggers from the body.

These associations can be further clarified and described. The part that triggers an emotion is called a reactionary cause, because it is an emotional reaction to some cause which triggers it. An example of a reactionary cause would be seeing a spider and feeling fear. The spider has been a cause for the activation of fear; the fear here is a reaction to the spider. Moreover the person did not choose to activate the fear but it springs up as a reaction to the spider. Again an example of a reactionary cause could be someone seeing a slug and feeling disgust; the slug has triggered a feeling of disgust. The actionary hold is the other side of the association. The actionary hold is the investment of emotion that underpins the reactionary cause. Actionary because it is the opposite of a reaction; it is a stockpile of emotion built up with action. A hold because it holds onto/is associated with a particular thing. To return to the example, over time an investment of fear has taken place (the action) in the thing, spider, which allows for the reaction to take place. Similarly an investment of disgust has been built up in regards to slug with the other association. There is an investment of emotion such that the emotion can be triggered. The two sides of the emotional association are interdependent. The reactionary cause being the side of the association that is the emotional trigger, the actionary hold being the side of the association that is the underlying attachment of emotion to the associated thing. This further explains what has been described as an association.

Associations explain a lot of our normal psychic life. They explain why a person feels a certain way in a certain place or why that provokes them to anger and that provokes them to fear. The everyday hustle and bustle of the psyche is the result of these actionary holds/reactionary causes. For example a person wakes up in the morning and smells bacon cooking in the kitchen which triggers their want emotion; getting up they look out of the window and it's raining, which triggers their sorrow;

going downstairs they see their wife which triggers their love; checking through the morning mail they see a bill which triggers their anger; outside a car suddenly starts which triggers their fear. All these are the reactionary cause side of the association but we can add the actionary hold side as well. Long habit of having it for breakfast has made the smell of bacon an actionary hold of want; being unable to go out and play on rainy days as a child has led to rain being linked with sorrow; he loves his wife; ever increasing utility bills recently have made him get angry so the sight of a bill is developing into an anger actionary hold; from his sister jumping out at him as a child sudden loud noises have built up an association with fear. The reader themselves can check if this is so if they think over their day or even if they consider their emotional responses to this work. Most of our normal emotional activity comes from these actionary holds/reactionary causes. They explain why we feel like we do when experiencing everyday occurrences. A lot of our development comes from building up new ones or the lapse of old ones. For example a person may become less afraid because their fear is no longer being triggered at work because the boss who triggered that fear has gone.

A distinct type of association is habit. These are associations that have been built up through long repetition leading to automatic actions. Habit is that we have a trigger to do certain things, often at certain times. For example a habit of wiping one's feet after entering the house is a habit if it is done as an automatic reaction on entering the house. Similarly having a drink at eight o'clock at night could be a habit such that one is pouring the drink without even thinking about it. A habit is distinguished from a normal association by its being deeply ingrained.

Our emotions then do not operate in a void. They are attached to things and to people in a very important way. This can best be described as us being embedded in this world. Without the inter-action with the people and things around us our emotional life would be very different.

A group of associations is a complex, in the sense of a group centered on the same center. For example another person could be a complex, they evoke love, pity, anger, hate, a whole batch of emotions. Again a powerful emotional experience could lead to a joy complex, where the complex is a cluster of joy associations rather than a cluster of emotions around one thing. For example because of a very joyful wedding, cake could be associated with joy, champagne could, the music that had been played at the reception could etc.

Our associations are often picked up from society at large. I call this cultural baggage because it is the burden of associations passed onto us from the surrounding culture and not determined by ourselves. For example because surrounding society has a thing about women's breasts that sexual association can come about in a way it would not in another culture. Again associating smoking with respect could come from the surrounding culture. A historical example could be the Hitler youth being brought up to associate hate with the Jews. This is cultural baggage; it is picked up from one's culture not purely from individual experience.

Chapter 7

Memory

Memory is a specific type of actionary hold. In the sense of being an investment of emotion. For example the memory of seeing a plane crash at an air show is an emotional investment of fear. The fear was felt as the engines stuttered and the plane began to dive, and as the plane hit the ground in a ball of flame. This fear has been preserved/invested in a specific memory. As can be seen actionary holds themselves, in the sense of the previous chapter, are often built on memories. Thus the memory example of seeing the plane crash could lead to a fear of flying. The fear of seeing the plane crash has become an actionary hold of fear on planes which is triggered (reactionary cause) by flying on an airplane.

Experience shows there are a variety of types of memory. The most obvious is that of the specific episode, the memory of a bus ride with your dad, the memory of your first school dinner and how you could not eat the dessert, the memory of buying that pair of shoes. All these are remembered episodes. Another type of memory is that of being able to remember something like the details of a battle learned at school. This is not a memory of an episode, you may not even remember learning it, but you know it and can remember it. Another example would be remembering that green means go at a traffic light; you do not remember an episode rather you remember a piece of knowledge. A third type of memory is even more non-episodic as it is a type of capacity, like remembering how to ride a bike or tie up your shoelaces. Such remembered capacities are not recalled like the date of a battle but as remembering how to do something. What this work is interested in here is how these memories come about, and how emotions are involved in them.

One way a memory seems to come about is from a strong emotional occurrence. Experience shows this can create a memory. A strong emotional experience impresses itself on the memory. For example being woken up in the middle of the night by the fire alarm going off and the ensuing panic can impress itself on the memory, or the shattering moment when you were dumped by your boyfriend can. There seems to be a connection between strong emotional episodes and memory. Similarly experience shows weak emotional occurrences do not seem to last long in memory.

Another way a memory can come about is through repetition of the experience. If an experience is repeated it builds up an impression. It has been seen how repetition can build up an actionary hold, likewise it can build up a memory (which is a type of actionary hold). For example walking the same way to work can build up a memory of the way to work or repeated viewing of a film can build up a memory of its scenes. Walking to work only once, one might not remember the way exactly a second time around, but having walked that way several times it will probably be remembered exactly.

Experience shows that some people are better at remembering certain things. For example at school some people are better at remembering history and others are better at remembering science. This at least in part seems to be due to the emotional involvement, the person who remembers history well is usually more interested in history and vice versa. Some people also seem to have a natural capacity for remembering certain things while others do not. For example some people can remember maths very easily while other people struggle to hold onto it. Again some people pick up and remember grammar easily while others have to really work at it to remember it.

Imagination seems to be connected with memory. In the sense that it is playing and creating out of that which is remembered. For example imagining a fire would not be possible without remembering in some sense what a fire is. Or imagining a battle would not be possible without remembering things like soldiers and guns. What comes easily to imagination seems from experience to be that which is emotionally involving to that person. For example a person may find it very easy to imagine boats because they have a strong emotional involvement in them.

Chapter 8

Exercise

Experience shows emotions discharge if not used. That is they seek to be exercised. For example if a person feels no sorrow over anything for a long time they may become depressed which is a way of the emotion exercising. This appears very clearly with the sex drive if nothing stimulates it; it will discharge itself and probably build up a new association in doing so. Similarly, if one is not afraid for a time one will become afraid over something. All this shows how the emotions seek to be exercised, and that if they are not they will do it themselves by discharging. This provides further evidence that emotions need to be used to be maintained, so much so that they will exercise themselves when not used. This exercise explains a lot of the build-up of new associations; when the old ones are not stimulating the exercise of the emotion it will discharge and in so doing build up a new association. For example if nothing has stimulated the sex drive for a while it will seek stimulation and may find it in a new attraction.

The exercise of emotions throws an interesting light on dreams. Some dreams seem to be able to be explained in regards to emotions not having exercised themselves in waking life doing so in sleep instead. For example if no fear has been felt in waking life a nightmare might occur whereby the fear exercises itself.

Chapter 9

Conscious/Unconscious

The unconscious as such cannot be directly experienced but can be inferred from experience. As such it can be defined as that part of the psyche that cannot be observed directly by the self. The evidence for the existence of this part of the psyche are minute details of memory that can be recalled under hypnosis but not otherwise, dreams (particularly those inferred from seeing another person tossing and turning in sleep that the person on waking cannot remember, these are truly unconscious whereas those that can be remembered are those that have moved from unconsciousness into consciousness), and suppressed content which cannot be directly experienced while suppressed (and is thus unconscious then) but can become conscious afterwards. The unconscious then is the dark side of the psyche that we are only aware of when it is brought into the light.

Suppression has been brought up and needs explaining. Suppression is when one or more emotions suppresses a part of the psyche; what is suppressed can be a memory, an association, a complex or an entire emotion. The suppressed content becomes unconscious because it can no longer be perceived by the person, because its existence is being denied. There are two parts to suppression, one of denying the existence of the suppressed content so that it cannot be perceived and is thereby made unconscious. For example a man who does not want to be hateful denying he is hating people when he is; as such he cannot see his own hate, it has become unconscious. The second, more extreme, part of suppression being actively thrusting the suppressed content down with another emotion or emotions, such that whenever the content surfaces one suppresses it. This thrusting down is usually coupled with the denying, thereby making the content unconscious. For example if someone was sexually attracted to someone but did not want to be they might deny that attraction, and whenever the attraction was activated by the presence of the person (a reactionary cause), they thrust it down, denying it and trying not to feel it. The problem with suppression is that it sets one part of the psyche against another; the suppression is only maintained by pressure (in this sense it is a type of action conflict as it is one or more emotions in conflict over something) which itself causes tension within the psyche. Nor does suppression remove the content that has been suppressed. If it is only denied it will go on being felt; it will just be unconscious now (as unconscious it will not be subject to conscious control). For example the man who has suppressed his hate by denial continues to feel hate and thereby maintain it; he just no longer sees his hate. If the suppressed content is thrust down, it will still have had to become active to be thrust down, and it may exercise itself in order to become active. For example the person who thrusts down their attraction will have had to have felt the attraction in order to thrust it down, and they might find themselves dreaming of the person they are attracted to at night, or fantasizing about them by day in spite of themselves. Suppression then does not remove what it tries to remove, and creates tension in its attempt to do so.

Consciousness is that which can be observed directly by the self. As such it is not just what is being experienced now but anything that can be recalled at will as well. It can be broken down into two parts, the active which is that which is currently going on, and the inactive which is that which is not going on currently but can become active.

Chapter 10

Emotions in the Background

Sometimes emotions are experienced in a different way than usual. They are not active up front like usual but in the background. Our normal change of emotions is going on, but present as a backdrop to these is an emotion in the background. This emotion may have been triggered by something in particular, but they are not about anything in particular. If strong they can hinder the feeling of other emotions. The most clear example of this is depression; other emotions are going on like normal (even joy and amusement) but in the background and when the other emotions have subsided, sorrow is present, nor is this sorrow over something; it is just there. Another example would be someone being irritable in the sense that they do all their normal activities and associated emotions, but underlying all these is the emotion of anger that keeps showing itself; nor is this anger about something, it is just there. These emotions in the background can go on for a long time more or less strongly; thus someone might be depressed for weeks.

This seems to come about either as part of exercise, the emotion has discharged but instead of onto something specific in a general way it is in the background, or it can be triggered with a reactionary cause. These are the same emotions just experienced in a different way. Thus sorrow and depression are the same emotion.

Often when the emotion in the background passes a bounce back is experienced. The other emotions that have not been felt or have not had room to be felt strongly now exercise themselves when the emotion hogging the active has passed. This bounce back can even cause the end of the emotion being in the background, as other emotions build up to be discharged. The strong activation of other emotions can also bring an end to the emotion being in the background, as can removal of the triggers that are activating the emotion.

This brings up the phenomenon of emotional saturation. One can become saturated as far as the active is concerned and have no room left for other emotions because one or a group are taking up the active space. For example if one is strongly depressed one will not feel other emotions so strongly, and one will spend time feeling sorrow rather than other emotions. Or if one has had a very emotionally stimulating day come evening one may feel emotionally listless.

Saturation can result in boredom. Boredom is when the emotions are for a time not focused on any particular thing but flit from thing to thing not exercising strongly. This can come about because nothing is activating one's emotions strongly or because one is saturated so much that there is no room for new activation, and no emotions are seeking to be discharged. An example would be someone who has lots of potential activities that could interest them but does not feel like doing any of them, and complains of being bored.

Chapter 11

Molds

Experience shows that strong associations have more of an effect than just their association. They act as molds, influencing the shape the person's new associations will take. Strong associations influence the types of new associations that will be formed. Influencing what an emotion exercising itself will be likely to discharge on. These are called Molds because they shape other associations. For example if someone has a strong fear of spiders when they form new fear associations their fear will follow the flow of that Mold, so they may develop fears of similar things like insects or things that look like or move like spiders. When encountering new experiences, whether they react with fear will partly be determined by their previous fear Molds. Similarly if someone had a girlfriend where they found her butt very sexually stimulating they will not just be aroused by that butt but by butts that look like it. Again previous sexual partners and attractions will partly determine the kind of person that will be found attractive in the future; the key past ones forming Molds that will determine the future ones. If someone has a build-up of a new emotion but no current associations then it will discharge and that emotion will flow to things similar to the Molds. For example if someone has a build-up of worry it will flow to the Molds of worry or things similar to them. Thus if someone has a Mold of worry of enclosed spaces and has a build-up of worry it may discharge forming a new association with cars, because cars are enclosed.

These Molds are very important in a person's psychic life. They partly determine what direction the person's emotions will flow in the future, and what associations they are likely to build up. The first Molds built up as a child and adolescent will still be having an influence later in life. Partly not fully determine, because the emotions are able to build up new associations on pretty much anything, but they are much more likely to follow the Molds as a form of connection is already there, and it is the path of least resistance.

Chapter 12

Knowledge Emotions

There are two emotions that work differently to the other emotions. These are the knowledge emotions reason and belief. They work differently because as will be seen they build their associations in a different way. This different way creates what this work calls knowledge.

This does not mean knowledge in one sense is not gained from the other emotions. However, other emotions only form a raw kind of knowledge, that of direct experience. They encounter things and interact with things but do not reflect on them or build knowledge out of them.

The way reason and belief work differently is that instead of forming actionary holds (the emotional investment part of an association) they form structures. These are different to actionary holds because they are more interconnected to one another. They are more built like. They are composed of interlocking parts like a wooden box is made of planks. The reason or belief has not been invested on a thing but has woven itself on something. For example one might have an awe association with the color green, this is very different to having a reason structure about how the Cathars are not Manicheans. The reason structure is made up of interlocking components such as "the Cathars do not perform the ritual meal" and "the Cathar division is between body and spirit not light and dark", whereas the green association is simply green awe. Again a belief in Father Christmas is different to a joy association with Father Christmas; the belief has a structured form like "Father Christmas exists" and "delivers presents" (though not necessarily formally expressed in language like that). Whereas the joy association is less complex; it is a reaction of joy to the image of Father Christmas. If reason or belief were to discharge then, it would form a new structure, not a new actionary hold. The actionary hold can be compared to throwing a lump of mud onto something whereas the structure can be compared to throwing a net onto something. As can be seen the knowledge emotions reason and belief form associations in a different way to other emotions.

Just as the knowledge emotions do not form normal actionary holds, so they do not have normal reactionary causes (the emotional trigger side of an association). Instead of reacting like green awe or spider fear, their structures are touched on provoking reason or belief about them. For example if someone were to mention the Cathars a whole string of reasons about them might crop up, the structure has been touched on.

Nor do the knowledge emotions have Molds (strong associations that influence the forming of new associations) like other emotions. We do not form new knowledge out of the images of the old in the way we form new attractions or fears. Rather when developing new structures we usually build on top of the old. If one has a build-up of reason that discharges it will usually discharge in thought on existing structures and build an extension to them as it were; belief will do similar. For example if one is interested in science and in particular astronomy, if nothing has stimulated one's reason for a while and reason discharges, it will probably discharge in thinking about and adding to one's structures about astronomy. One might add a new structure on comets on top of the old structure as one thinks about it. An example for belief would be if one believes in a particular religion; if belief discharges it will usually discharge in renewed belief on that religion structure. The knowledge emotions then do not have Molds, but like the other emotions when they discharge and form new structures they will follow the path of least resistance and build on existing structures.

When reason and belief are in action conflict (where they pull in different directions over the same action) this is a particular type of action conflict called doubt. Such a conflict can lead either to suppression of one side or the forming of agreement between the two emotions (as well as dissolution, of course, if the circumstances change). For example one could reason the theory of evolution while at the same time not believing it and thus be in a state of doubt about it. Or one could believe in the Conservative party but have rational misgivings about them, and thus be in doubt over them.

As reason and belief are emotions this raises the question how is one able to come to sound knowledge, since the knowledge emotions are subjective? That is they are the fallible product of a particular subject, namely a human being, therefore they can be mistaken about how things really are. That they are subjective is shown by the experience that if you give two unbiased people the same set of data they can still both reason different conclusions. Knowledge must therefore be accepted as something subjective but within a subject it can be more or less sound. One way of making it sound is for there to be no doubt; in other words for reason and belief to agree on it. Another way is for the reason and belief felt about the structure in question to be strong not weak. A third more objective criteria is for the structure to be centered on direct experience (particularly the primordial experience of emotions), not on second-hand report or imaginative experience. When it matches these three things, experience centered, strong, not doubtful, it is called truthed by this work. This truth is still subjective but it is strong and grounded in experience.

Reason stands out from the other emotions because it has its own form of experience. Which I call reflection. Other emotions encounter things (whether now or remembered) but reason reflects on things. This reflection is a reasoning chewing over, it is experiencing by reasoning.

Chapter 13

Meditation

Emotions do not need an object. Experience shows that I can just love without loving something. Again one can just be afraid without being afraid of something. So it is with all emotions. Grammar insists that a proper sentence has an object as well as a subject but experience shows that our feelings do not have to conform to grammar. It is possible to say, "I worry", because one does worry without worrying about anything in particular. I have noticed that some people have a problem with this and demand that it is not possible to have an emotion without an object. I can only say again that that is true only in regards to good grammar, not actual life. The best thing for the reader to do is test this for themselves by their own experience.

Nor is it just that we can experience emotions without an object. We can do so at will. This is shown by repeated experience. The reader can test this for themselves if they try to feel worried or frightened without being worried or frightened about anything specific. If one finds this difficult one can imagine reactionary causes, like imagining a person one loves, and feeling love for them. With practice it becomes easier to shift from imagining something one loves to just feeling love. This work calls this capacity meditation; this is not to be confused with any religious mode of meditation. Moreover experience shows that the capacity to meditate improves with repeated use.

What this capacity to meditate means for the psyche is that we are able to abstract ourselves from the uncontrolled hustle and bustle of normal emotional stimulation (that is reactionary causes and involuntary exercise). Meditation also further shows how the emotions are not bound up with any particular actions, as they do not even need an object to be felt over.

Chapter 14

The Self

Preconceived notions of the self need to be discarded. This description of the self is not based on the I. Rather it is self as in self-control. The capacity as shown from meditation to activate one's emotions. The capacity to do that is called the self in this work.

Experience shows that emotions can be activated at will. The reader can check this for themselves like in the last chapter. Further investigation reveals more about what this capacity of self is. The capacity of self is not simply like an on/off switch for the emotions; the experience is more complex than that. Rather the self is like having a remote control for the emotions without the off button; we can change from one emotion to another but not turn the emotions off. Nor is it as easy as pressing the button on a remote control. In order to use the self an emotion is needed to press the button as it were. This is the emotion that will be switched to. For example if one is feeling rational one can change to feeling love. The self has activated love and this has pushed reason out of the active. The self is this capacity to change what one is feeling but has no power to do this on its own. Experience shows that the emotion used by the self to replace the currently active emotion must be strong enough in comparison with it to do so. However, experience also shows that the newly active emotion need not be stronger. For example if a person feels lots of anger they can use the self to switch to guilt and that feeling of guilt that replaces the anger need not feel more intense than the anger it replaces. Experience shows that sometimes the currently active emotion will be too strong for the emotion used with the self to replace it. For example if a person is feeling very afraid and tries to replace that fear with anger they may not succeed in doing so. Experience shows emotions in the background are particularly difficult to shift because they are not in the active, but active underneath so to speak.

The self is also that particular group of emotions under that self's control. In other words the individual. The self represents that distinct holding together of that person's emotions, which that person can potentially activate with their self.

This distinct batch of emotions is held together through time and yet it remains the same self even though the strength of the emotions changes. Not only this, but the four categories of emotions are held together in the individual even though two of them are in permanent conflict. Moreover these different categories can even change channels with one another. This means that the self of animals will be different simply because they do not have a self made up of the four categories. The human self is thus distinctly human.

Chapter 15

Example

In order to illustrate the dynamics of the psyche a brief fictional example will be gone through now. Not a full account of a life but a sketch. The example is John, a thirty-five-year-old man. An account of his development and current psychic life will be given.

At birth John's emotional make-up was that he was strong in hate, the sex drive, curiosity, respect, and pity, weak in anger, cruelty, reason, guilt and awe. The other emotions were of medium strength when compared with those named. This raises the question of what at birth determines our emotional heritage. Experience shows that sometimes children are emotionally like their parents to a noticeable degree. On the other hand experience also shows children can be emotionally different to the parents. For example two parents strong in reason have a daughter strong in reason but a son that is not. One would expect some form of heredity to go on, but unlike bodily features it is much harder to test where the emotional make-up is hereditary and where developed because one cannot ask the child at birth.

John quickly forms associations with the things around him. Want with sweets. Disgust with broccoli. Respect for his father. Fear of his mother. Love of his mother. Curiosity with the garden which he explores. John quickly becomes emotionally embedded in the world around him.

In the first few years of life John builds up his first Molds. As very few memories of early life remain most of these have to be inferred backwards from his behavior as a child. John is afraid of rats; though he has no memory of a bad experience with rats, he remembers being afraid of rats since at least the age of four. A particular complex of Molds is centered around football. This comes about from the influence of his dad, who is a strong football fan. John remembers from a young age being taken to watch football matches; these were emotionally intense occasions and John remembers them well. As such John has a complex of two Molds with football: one of curiosity and one of amusement. It is these strong early associations with football that will be the basis of him developing an interest in other sports when he is older.

The first major emotional change in John's life is that hate ceases to be a strong emotion in him when compared with the other emotions; it has diminished. This is because hate has built up very few associations; yes it has exercised itself and built up some but John has activated it himself very little. Thus by age four John's hate has diminished.

As John progresses through primary school other associations develop and some associations lose their power. The first sexual association he remembers is when he had a crush on a girl in his class at age six. It did not last long nor was it very strong so it did not become a Mold. At age eight John sees an air show and as a result of the awe filled and joyous experience develops making model planes as a hobby. Bullied at age nine by another boy John develops an association of respect with force. By age ten due to changing tastes John's association of disgust with broccoli has gone. At age eleven his grandmother dies leaving John to associate sorrow with flowers as they are placed on her grave, and a mix of love and sorrow for hymns as she used to sing them to him and he both loved her and grieves over her loss.

In John's teenage years John forms the Molds that will be key to who he finds attractive in later life. Due to the surrounding culture he develops a sex drive Mold with large breasts. A strong crush on a blonde girl in the year above at school leads to a Mold with her. Blondes and women who look like her will be attractive to John in later life. Similarly a long-term relationship with another blonde from sixteen to eighteen will create a Mold with her. The unhappy break-up will make the association more complex as the association will be both one of hate and desire.

During his teenage years John's emotional make-up changes. Pity diminishes and curiosity and the sex drive become even stronger. All again due to lack or growth in stimulation.

Other important associations from this period include a guilt association with maths and an anger association with swimming. Guilt becomes associated with maths because John is not very good at it and his teacher berates him and ridicules him about it. The association of anger with swimming comes about because he is frustrated at not being competent at it unlike the other sports he plays. He has a major action conflict over doing homework; on the one hand reason and guilt urge him to do it and do it well, while on the other hand curiosity and amusement urge him to make plane models, watch TV etc. This action conflict crops up throughout his school years whenever he has homework to do. It is sometimes resolved by John exercising his self for the side his reason is invested in, even though it is felt weaker than his amusement and curiosity.

At age eighteen John joins the air force to train as a pilot. Respect forms new associations with his superiors, a number of relationships with women bring associations but not Molds as they are brief. Joy and curiosity are associated with flying. Fear with the air force's war games. Kindness with another recruit he helps. Disgust with the horror movies his friends watch. Vanity with his car.

At twenty-five John leaves the air force and becomes a commercial pilot, leading to a break with his air force associations and new associations forming with his changing life. For the first year of being a commercial pilot John often suffers from boredom as, until new associations build up to replace the very large investment he had in the air force, little stimulates his emotions. John also has very vivid dreams at this time, possibly as his emotions exercise themselves on their own. He left the air force because he believed and reasoned he will get more money as a commercial pilot; experience shows this to be right. John is greedy for money. At twenty-six John marries an air hostess he met while working; she looks similar to the girl he fell in love with at eighteen. Their marriage is stormy; John has a lot of emotional investment in her ranging from hate and anger to love and pity. Though his wife has strong sex drive associations, driven by his strong curiosity and sex drive John has numerous affairs with other women which become a strong vanity association. John also feels worried about these affairs but suppresses the worry; he feels the worry over them but would not admit to it if asked, and tries to stop himself feeling it.

Now John is thirty-five his emotional make-up has changed, and the things his emotions are associated with have come and gone. He is now strong in vanity, the sex drive, respect and curiosity, and weak in anger, cruelty, guilt and awe. This then has been a brief fictional illustration of how this work conceives of the functioning of the human psyche.

Part III

Psyche

Chapter 16

Psyche

Experience shows that we experience everything with the emotions. Our knowledge, our daily lives, our interactions with things and people are conducted with what this work calls emotion. We encounter nothing without feeling emotion even if very weak. Even the experience of our senses is received emotionally. That is our sense experience does not matter until it is picked up by the emotions. For example I may see a bus coming towards me but it does not matter or get taken up by me until I respond to it emotionally, by in joy realizing that's my bus or in fear that it's about to hit me etc.

This raises the question what is sense experience of? And with this, does it differ from emotional experience? It seems that we have two modes of experience; the primordially emotional (that is direct and unmediated), and the sensual. The sensual is emotional as well but not primordially in the way direct experience of the emotions is. The sensual gives us the experience of other things whereas the primordially emotional is of our own self (the primordially emotional is experience of unmediated emotions whereas the sensual is of emotions mediated via the senses). What then do the senses experience? They give us experience of other things and since we only experience them emotionally they are experiences of emotions. That is, when I see that bus coming towards me, I am seeing not a bus made of matter that I experience with my mental emotions but a bus made of emotions. There are two realms of emotional experience, the sensual and the primordially emotional. Both the sensual and the primordially emotional are experience of and by emotions. They differ in providing two different kinds of experience, like hearing provides a different mode of experiencing things to sight. What then is the body? It is part of your self as it can be controlled by you; it is part of that distinct holding together that distinguishes your emotions from other emotions. The body is experienced by the senses, and is itself the part of the self that allows sense experience (it has the eyes, the ears etc.). The body is then the interface between our primordial emotions and the sensual realm; if it is damaged the access to the sensual realm could also be damaged.

This is not to say that these sense experiences are all in our minds and have no existence outside of us, but rather to say that they are experiences of other emotions outside our immediate self. They are not part of ourselves as they are not experienced primordially nor are they under our self-control; rather they are independent. I call this position Psychicalism to distinguish it from Idealism (Idealism being the position in philosophy that there is no physical world, it is all in our mind). The experience of the senses is not all in our minds; rather it is all of minds. The table that I see before me is not in my mind, rather it is another independent mind, emotion separate from myself. Of what emotion then is the table? Is it a table that is of hate or anger or love? Given that animals do not show good and evil but they are only experienced by humans one would not expect the table to be of them. Also not all animals show the neutral emotions; some do not seem to show reason or guilt etc. The only category that remains to all and therefore could compose that which is experienced sensually is nature. The sensual realm is the realm of nature. To return to the example of the table which is another mind, it can be conceived as part of the natural mind of the world. The table, the chairs, the walls of the room are all part of the psyche that is the natural world, and can be thought of as one natural psyche.

Chapter 17

The Collective Unconscious

As everything is psyche we are all one substance. Not only that but we share the same categories of emotions. I may be a distinct group of emotions but my fellow human beings have the same emotions. Not only that but we have the same categories (natural and neutral) as animals and the sensual world (natural). This suggests the possibility of a higher union.

We have experience of things that suggest some form of higher union. We can sometimes read the moods of people we know well even though their body language does not suggest it. We have the experience of being swept up in a crowd's emotion, of passing on the mood to one another. Like being swept up in the atmosphere of a concert. We have experience of strange coincidences that are yet meaningful[2], like thinking for the first time in years of an old friend and then getting an unexpected call from them. We also have experience in dreams that might suggest a connectedness, like dreaming of escaping from a prison camp and the next day finally being discharged from hospital. All this is evidence of a connectedness.

These experiences show a connection between us and each other that is beyond the sensual connection. We are all one psyche, distinct yet of the same substance. The table I see is another mind but it is also a part of the universal psyche, as am I. The Collective Unconscious[3] is this universal psyche. It is Collective as it is universal; it is Unconscious as it is not directly accessible to us but sometimes reveals itself through the evidence cited. The explanation of the evidence is that we can pick up the emotions of others because they are part of our Collective Unconscious; we are part of each other so we can sometimes know or be influenced by (like the emotion from the crowd) others. The reason why people more familiar to us are more easily picked up is because we are more connected (with associations) to them, thus it is easier for them to pass into our consciousness.

There is the self which is our personal consciousness and personal unconscious (the parts of our self that we cannot directly perceive like the suppressed), and there is the Collective Unconscious which is everything. We are part of the Collective Unconscious, and it is part of us. The table which I see is not only another mind, but part of my mind via the Collective Unconscious, and I am part of its mind via the Collective Unconscious. Via the Collective Unconscious everything is connected, and everything is one while still having its distinct self.

Chapter 18

Life after Death

If the world is psyche rather than physical this raises the question can we live in some form without our sensual bodies? For if my self is not dependant on the body then there is the possibility it will go on without my body. It needs to be seen whether the self is dependant on the body or not.

We can experience all our emotions via purely emotional experience. The four categories of emotion give us the distinct human self. The self is not only as in self-control but as in this distinct cluster of emotions differentiated from the Collective Unconscious. As we have experience of all four categories that make up the self without the sensual, and as the self is the description of what distinguishes us, there is the possibility that we can exist without the sensual. For if the sensual is not a necessary part of our selves we may continue without it. That is live on after the death of the body.

Emotional experience is primordial whereas sense experience is not. One may be mistaken about the object of an emotion or quibble over the name of it but the actual direct feeling of emotion is unfiltered and primordial. Whereas sense experience may be mistaken, or even like hallucinations not from the senses as such. This suggests the primacy of primordially emotional experience over sensual experience. Suggesting that we may survive beyond the senses.

Energy does not simply disappear. If emotional energy is not dependant on the body it will probably not disappear with the body. Experience shows that the energy of emotions comes from use, not the body. This suggests that the primordially emotional can go on without the sensual. Once again suggesting life after death might be possible.

All of this evidence combined: the sensual not being a necessary part of the self, emotional experience being primordial, the energy of emotions possibly not being dependant on the body, suggests that life after death is a likely possibility. If this is so what would life after death be like? For a start without the body there would be no sensual experience. There would only be primordially emotional experience. If I were to go on without my body I would be able to feel my emotions, but not be able to see, touch, hear, taste, or smell. One would expect one would still have memory and imagination as they are not dependant on the senses.

Is the sensual possibly in some sense superfluous? That is if the emotional is not dependant upon the sensual is the sensual unnecessary and undesirable. The sensual is not superfluous. The sensual provides the stimulation and thus the growth of our everyday lives. Through the sensual we build up associations with other people and things. Without it we would have much greater difficulty growing emotionally.

Part IV

Freedom

Chapter 19

Self-Control

Meditation, that is the capacity to self activate an emotion, has shown that we can have some self-control over our emotions. For example we can become angry without any stimulus from a reactionary cause. We can experience our emotions as and when we choose using meditation.

This capacity for meditation allows a degree of freedom. By taking control of when we activate our emotions we are free from having their activation determined by reactionary causes (things that trigger an emotion). This is not to say that the reactionary causes will stop stimulating emotions but that we can change to a different emotion if we want, thereby having some control over what we feel. Use of meditation allows a freedom from being determined by our own associations.

As already mentioned the capacity for this kind of self-control improves with use. The more frequently meditation is used the easier it becomes to use. And the greater the ability to be free from the compulsion of reactionary causes. Indeed experience shows that if an emotion gets its use from meditation such that it no longer seeks to exercise itself, it becomes abstracted from its reactionary causes.

Experience shows there are limitations to this capacity from meditation for self-control. Emotions that are experienced very strongly are harder to switch off, and emotions in the background like depression go on underneath the normal hustle and bustle of emotional life and cannot be switched off. Also an emotion that is unconscious cannot be subject to self-control. Experience shows that controlling these types of emotion that are harder to control with meditation can be controlled to a certain extent by focusing on their triggers (their reactionary causes). This is done by confronting the triggers. Confronting is when you allow the reactionary cause to trigger the emotion and stick with it (that is not fleeing from the trigger) until the emotion has gone down. If one flees from the trigger the association will remain associated with the strong emotion, whereas if one stays the association will be with the emotion when it is less intense. An illustration will help explain this. A type of music triggers a very large amount of worry. If when the music is heard the person flees; the association will remain with the initial intense feeling of worry. However, if the person stays until the music passes of its own accord, it will be associated with the more subsided feeling of worry. Repetition will make the association weaker. The emotion which is too strong to meditate away can thereby be controlled by reducing its triggers so that things do not stimulate it to that strong level.

Chapter 20

Passivity

Passivity is here meant not just in the sense of being passive and doing nothing, but also in the sense of doing something when the urge is to not. For example if one's normal action (that is the action associated with the emotion) is to lash out when angry, passivity here would mean not lashing out. On the other hand if one's normal action when afraid is to be routed to the spot, passivity here would be to act. This passivity is a freedom from action, being able to choose how one acts rather than having it determined by one's associations.

This passivity can be developed through meditation. Instead of controlling the emotion one is controlling the associated action. This is developed by calling up the emotion through meditation and then not doing the associated action, thereby developing the freedom to choose one's actions. For example if when someone feels curious they have to have a look, then one could call up the feeling of curiosity with meditation and allow oneself to experience the feeling without doing anything. One thereby reduces the association of having to look by not doing it. Passivity is also practiced when one experiences an emotion triggered by a reactionary cause and remains passive. Like if one is afraid of snakes and sees a grass snake but does not run, and instead continues with the gardening one was doing as normal.

Part V

Ethics

Chapter 21

Ethics

The basis of ethics is already present in this work. There are two categories of emotion called good and evil. The ethics is to be good not evil. To end the conflict between good and evil in one's psyche, completely if possible. The evidence for the ability to totally remove evil is that it is possible for emotions to diminish, and that certain historical figures appear to be free from evil. The experience of the ability to diminish emotions raises the possibility that they can be totally removed, as does the experience that some people can seem to lack an emotion. This would be better confirmed by first-hand experience. The evidence of historical figures is of course removed from first-hand experience but adds to the likelihood of the possibility. If an emotion could be removed it would not be able to come back as it would no longer be there to be activated, so it would not be able to grow.

Good and evil is more than a personal thing. It is something we have experience from other people who have the same emotional categories as us. As part of the Collective Unconscious all that good (as well as the other categories) is connected. Life after death also raises the question, where do we go if we continue? Similarly other animals lacking good and evil begs the question, where does it come from in humans? The other two categories, neutral and natural, exist outside human beings, especially nature in the sensual world. All this points to good and evil existing outside of human beings as well. This good outside of us is God, as God is good. This is not God in the sense of the classical God but in the sense of all that is good, love and faith etc. As all the good is connected so it is all God. We have good in us so we have God in us. The same is so of the other categories.

There is a devil that is the sum of all that is evil, and a nature, and a neutral. There is also this pool of psychic energy as was said earlier. One would expect that the emotions outside of us draw on this pool of formless energy as well in order to grow and be maintained.

The existence of God and the devil outside of human beings potentially solves the question of where we go after death. No longer being anchored in the sensual we are pulled to the category of either good or evil that we have the most of. Meaning we are pulled into the presence of this outside of us good or this outside of us evil, that is into the presence of God or the devil. I do not think we are pulled to nature because that is mainly the sensual, or to nature or neutral because they do not have this conflict like good and evil that attracts and repels. The realm of good can be given its traditional name of heaven; there one would be surrounded by an intense love and the other good feelings. In heaven one would be surrounded by the realm of goodness experienced primordially not second-hand like with the senses in the realm of nature. The good feelings of God would therefore penetrate one strongly; one would have an intense feeling of being loved etc. The realm of evil can be given its traditional name of hell; there one would be surrounded by an intense hate and the other evil emotions. Again primordially so one would feel very hated etc. This is of course different to the traditional picture of heaven and hell; there would be no physical torment or delight as there would be no body, there would be an intense and penetrating feeling though, so much so that it would probably stifle one's own growth. This means that we need to make a choice in this life to be either good or evil as that will determine where we go upon death. I do not think that our growth continues after death as if it did we could swap between heaven and hell, and there is no sensual stimulation. Maintenance would need to continue otherwise we would diminish and eventually disappear. Heaven and hell then would be like warehouses of the good or evil grown in humans on earth.

There will then not only be conflict between good and evil in the human psyche but outside of it as well. This raises the question of why does one side not destroy the other, and how will this conflict be resolved? There must be some kind of balance in strength between good and evil, otherwise one would expect the stronger to have destroyed the weaker. This means if one grows sufficiently the other would probably be destroyed. If such were to happen in the future one or other of good and evil would cease to be. This would be a radical change in the constitution of the world leading either to the elimination of good or evil.

How then is one to become more good and less evil? The answer is through meditation. By activating good emotions as much as possible with meditation one grows the amount of good in one. That is one draws on raw psychic energy and turns it into good. This will diminish the amount of evil by building up the amount of good such that good will become more active and the evil will not have room to be so active, and thus will diminish. Simply suppressing the evil will not reduce it as it makes it unconscious not inactive. Similarly trying to not activate evil by immediately switching to another emotion when one experiences it will mean that it discharges instead. Removing the evil from one's psyche is a long process about being good. As one increases in good so the level of good in the world is also increased. This means by being good you are not only becoming better yourself but helping the world to become better, and as part of the Collective Unconscious being better will affect others too. As the world becomes better a worldwide imbalance in favor of good over evil would happen, and if the imbalance were to reach a critical amount evil would be destroyed by good. Being good then also helps further the imbalance in God's favor, thereby helping bring about the total destruction of evil with God's victory over it.

This means that this ethics is not based on action but on being.

Only feeling good emotions makes one good in this sense, no action can. This ethics is based on building up our good emotions no matter what we do. Nor is ethics about motivating actions with goodness but about the amount of good emotion we have in us, not what it motivates us to do.

Chapter 22

Delusion

Delusion is believing/reasoning something that is not real. Like believing in unicorns, or thinking one is a good hockey player when one is not, or believing someone loves you when all the signs point to them not doing so. Delusion is also when one attaches too much importance to something that is trivial. Like attaching too great an importance to a game, or to money.

The problem with delusion is that it hinders one from being free and good. It hinders freedom by attaching too great an importance to things and actions that do not deserve that importance. For example attaching too great an importance to football such that one never controls the reactionary causes/actionary holds invested in it. It hinders being good by wasting time on unimportant things or things that are imaginary, where instead one could spend the time becoming better. As such it is part of ethics to overcome delusion so that one can be free to pursue goodness.

The way delusion is overcome is by truthing. That is by testing one's structures with belief and reason, such that they are in agreement and strong, and by keeping one's knowledge structures experience centered. It is not enough though just to recognize a delusion; one must also realize that it is a delusion in life. That is one must stop doing it. For example truthing that the number thirteen being unlucky is a delusion is not fully overcome until one actually stops avoiding the number thirteen. Truthing does not provide absolute objective knowledge; we could then never be certain we are free of delusion. However, we can by truthing be more certain if not absolutely certain.

Chapter 23

The Four Goals

There are four goals of ethics. That is four things to aim to become.

1. Tranquility
The first and most important goal is tranquility, that is freedom from primordial conflict by becoming good and rooting out evil (becoming good being the most important part of ethics), as well as not having the other type of conflict of suppression. This goal is achieved through mediating the good and hunting out and realizing one's suppressions.

2. Self-Control
The second goal is self-control, that is not being a slave to one's reactions. This also helps the first goal as greater self-control allows a greater capacity for good meditation. This second goal is achieved through meditation.

3. Passivity
The third goal is passivity, that is not being a slave to one's actions. Being able to choose whether to do or not to do. Once again this helps the first goal as it allows one to get on with the business of being good no matter the situation, as one does not have to give in to doing or not doing. This is also achieved through meditation.

4. Non-Delusion
The fourth goal is non-delusion, so that one is not hindered in being good or free. This is achieved by truthing (strong

experience centered reason and belief in agreement).

Thus there are four goals: tranquility, self-control, passivity and non-delusion.

Achievement of the four goals is called purity. As one is cleansed of evil, slavery and delusion. If one becomes pure one will of course be drawn by one's goodness to heaven upon death. Also by eliminating the evil in one's psyche one will no longer be plugged into the evil part of the Collective Unconscious, as one will no longer have that emotional category. Becoming pure also helps bring about the triumph of good over evil by wiping out the part of evil that is in one's self and increasing in good, thereby increasing the good of the entire world. Beyond being pure there is a higher goal, that of being a Champion of God. A Champion of God is where one increases the goodness in one's own psyche to a very high level, such even that one has the strength of goodness of a hundred normal people. The purpose of being a Champion of God is to help bring about God's victory over evil by increasing the amount of good in the world, thereby bringing about an imbalance in favor of good in the world, thus hopefully helping to bring about the total destruction of evil. This goodness of course is the good emotions within not any actions.

Part VI

Relations

Chapter 24

Solidarity

Alienation from others and from the natural world is unhelpful. Alienation in the sense of having a lack of emotional connection through associations with them. On the one hand being free from dependence on associations is desirable, but having few associations or none is not. Being alienated is unhelpful because the lack of connections means a lack of stimulation from reactionary causes, which leads to uncontrolled exercise and even the diminishing of one's emotions. For example if the sex drive is not being stimulated by anything because of alienation from people and things it will discharge on whatever it can in an uncontrolled fashion, therefore potentially building up a new association that is unwanted or frowned upon by society. The lack of connections also affects one's capacity to pick up the vibrations of the Collective Unconscious as one is not connected to people and nature, thus not plugged in so as to be receptive. As the Collective Unconscious is part of ourselves, by being alienated we are being alienated not just from others but from ourselves. Alienation then leads to a lack of control of one's emotions and the potential diminishing of one's emotions, which makes it unhelpful to being good.

In order to avoid alienation one must be in solidarity with people and with nature so that one has connections to them. Solidarity with people is achieved by having relationships with them, whether friendships, work relationships etc. thereby allowing the build-up of associations and thus emotional connections to them. Merely seeing other people with your eyes is not a proper connection as you do not encounter them as another full person, nor are you allowing much room to build up associations. Solidarity with the non-human around us is achieved by connecting with it (building up associations), whether by taking a walk in it or planting some plants etc. Solidarity is then having living emotional connections. Having old associations that are not stimulated anymore is no longer being connected, thus not being in solidarity.

Chapter 25

Freedom

This is freedom not in the emotional sense of self-control and passivity but in the social sense of being free to form relationships and be connected to one's fellow human beings and nature. That is sensual freedom, the freedom to act in the sensual world without constraint from others. For example if someone is locked up in a jail they are not free to meet and form relationships with those outside. In order to avoid alienation it is important to be able to meet and form relationships. Any constraint that hinders such freedom, like freedom of assembly, is unhelpful in avoiding alienation.

Chapter 26

Auxiliary Ethics

To be connected we need to be in solidarity with others and nature. If we are not it hinders our capacity to be self-controlled. Thereby hindering our ability to become pure.

The best form of solidarity is one that helps us to be good or gives us the opportunity to be good. The best form of this is one that is mutual where each person helps the other to be good. Mutual aid[4] in being good. This aid is not just that of stimulating the good emotions but of helping each other to combat delusion and gain self-control etc. This aid also extends to helping others to live thereby giving them the opportunity to be good. Thus providing food and health care is part of this aid.

This means there is an auxiliary ethics to the main ethics of being good. An action based ethic that plays a supporting role to the main ethics, and of course being based on actions not emotions is nowhere near as important. This supporting ethic is not being good but being helpful. Helpful meaning assisting others to be good or have the opportunity to be good. Assisting as in teaching or persuading (not forcing, as that would violate the other person's freedom). Providing the opportunity as in providing the continued life for the other person to have the opportunity to be good. An example would be providing food to the starving and shelter to the homeless, such that they do not die and cease to have the opportunity to be good. Another example would be helping someone to overcome their delusions or two people mutually helping one another to be good. The best kind of relationship to have with people, and that should be cultivated, is that of being mutually helpful. An ideal relationship would be mutually helpful towards being good, and free with no element of coercion or dominance by either person. This also means there are unhelpful acts and relationships. Killing someone and thereby preventing any good growth is unhelpful; it would rob them of all opportunities to grow in goodness. Similarly constraining someone so that they are hindered in exercising their emotions as they want by preventing them from speaking or torturing them is unhelpful. There is also not being helpful, that is having the opportunity to be helpful and not doing so. For example, having the food to feed someone who is starving but not doing so is not being helpful. There is an auxiliary ethic then to that of being good, namely being helpful; it is only an auxiliary ethic as doing any actions can never be a substitute for being good (no actions can admit one to heaven or bring about God's victory over evil).

Chapter 27

Anarchist Communism

With regards to others it has been shown that it is desirable to be in mutually helpful relationships and to be free. It is also desirable to be free of delusion. Attaching too much importance to money or commodities at the expense of being good is a delusion. Money itself only has the value we give to it; it has no value in itself and to treat it like it does is a delusion. Law is a delusion as they are just rules made by men, attaching importance to this fiction such that people die for or are locked away because of it is delusional. The state and rulers take away our freedom by deciding for us, and coercing us. To attach too much importance to anything other than being good is delusional.

There is only one form of politics that does not constrict freedom, allows helpful solidarity, and does not promote the delusions of money and law. This is anarchist communism. Anarchy meaning without the constraints of law, state or rulers, thereby free. Communism meaning being part of a mutually supportive community. As we become better and free of delusion so politically we will become anarchist communists. To force anarchist communism on people would violate their freedom, and to promote it by force would be unhelpful. Rather it is something to be evolved towards as more people free themselves from delusion.

Endnotes

1   Primordial is a term borrowed from Macquarrie and Robinson's translation of Heidegger's *Being and Time*, though with a slightly different use to that of Heidegger's.
2   Which C.G. Jung calls synchronicity.
3   The writings on the Collective Unconscious would not have been possible without reading C.G. Jung; none the less this work's take on the Collective Unconscious is different to Jung's.
4   A great work on a different but related form of mutual aid can be found in Kropotkin's *Mutual Aid*.

B O O K S

O is a symbol of the world, of oneness and unity. In different cultures it also means the "eye," symbolizing knowledge and insight. We aim to publish books that are accessible, constructive and that challenge accepted opinion, both that of academia and the "moral majority."

Our books are available in all good English language bookstores worldwide. If you don't see the book on the shelves ask the bookstore to order it for you, quoting the ISBN number and title. Alternatively you can order online (all major online retail sites carry our titles) or contact the distributor in the relevant country, listed on the copyright page.

See our website www.o-books.net for a full list of over 500 titles, growing by 100 a year.

And tune in to myspiritradio.com for our book review radio show, hosted by June-Elleni Laine, where you can listen to the authors discussing their books.

mySpiritRadio